Other titles in the series:

David Beckham
Rob Apps
978 0 7496 8232 3

Monty Panesar

Hope Powell

978 ... 35 4

For my nephew Matthew Layson

First published in 2008 by
Franklin Watts
338 Euston Road
London NW1 3BH

Franklin Watts Australia
Level 17/207 Kent Street
Sydney NSW 2000

Text © Roy Apps 2008
Illustrations © Chris King 2008
Cover design by Peter Scoulding

A CIP catalogue record for this book
is available from the British Library.

ISBN: 978 0 7496 8233 0

Dewey Classification: 796.72'092

1 3 5 7 9 10 8 6 4 2

Printed in Great Britain

Franklin Watts is a division of Hachette Children's Books,
an Hachette Livre UK company.
www.hachettelivre.co.uk

**Essex County
Council Libraries**

Lewis Hamilton

Roy Apps

Illustrated by Chris King

FRANKLIN WATTS
LONDON•SYDNEY

Chapter One:

The Christmas Present

Lewis looked out of the kitchen window and frowned. Weird things were happening at the bottom of the garden. Over the last few weeks his dad's shed had grown. There was a new end and brand new double doors along one side.

His dad was out in the shed now, but just what he was doing there Lewis had no idea. When he asked Linda, his step-mum, she said:

"Your grandad's coming to stay and we thought he might like to sleep in the shed, so your dad's fixing it up with a shower and loo."

Lewis knew she was joking. The shed was where Lewis's dad tested and repaired the remote-control cars that Lewis raced. Lewis was a champion remote-control car racer. He'd even been on *Blue Peter*. He was hoping to get a brand new remote-control car for Christmas.

Lewis spent Christmas Eve and the early part of Christmas morning with his mum, then she drove him a few streets over to his dad and step-mum's.

"Have a great day, Lewis!" she called.

"You too, Mum," yelled Lewis.

He rang the doorbell. There was no answer.

"Dad!" he shouted. "Linda?" Still no answer.

He bent down and peered through the letterbox. He couldn't see his dad or step-mum. What he could see, though, was a huge Christmas present out in the kitchen. Lewis's heart skipped a beat. Even with all that wrapping paper it was obviously a go-kart.

He stepped back from the door just as his dad and step-mum came up the side path. They'd been out for a walk with Nic, Lewis's baby half-brother.

"Hi, Lewis! Happy Christmas!" they both said, grinning like mad.

"Happy Christmas!" said Lewis.

When they got into the kitchen, Lewis didn't want to let them know he'd already seen his present through the letterbox, so he said:

"Wow! What is that?"

"It's a puppy, son," replied his dad. "A real whopper, isn't it?"

Lewis knew his dad was winding him up.

"Don't tease the boy, Anthony," said his step-mum. "Go on Lewis, open your present!"

Lewis ripped off the paper.

The go-kart was second hand and a bit battered, but it had been cleaned, polished and repaired. For a moment, Lewis was so excited, he was lost for words.

His dad and step-mum looked at each other with a frown. "It's what you wanted, isn't it, Lewis?" his step-mum asked.

Lewis's face spread into a massive grin. "More than anything in the world!" he whispered excitedly.

Chapter Two:

The Crash

"So now you know why I've been making the shed bigger," said Lewis's dad. "I couldn't see why we shouldn't keep your go-kart in the kitchen, next to the fridge, but Linda wouldn't hear of it."

"Too right, I wouldn't!" Linda laughed.

"Can we go real go-kart racing, Dad? Can we?"

"OK, but if you're going to do it, then you're going to do it properly."

"Of course I'll do it properly. I'm going to be the next Ayrton Senna," replied Lewis. Ayrton Senna was the most famous racing driver of the time: the McLaren team's number one driver, a three-times Formula 1 World Champion and Lewis's all-time hero.

Lewis's step-mum laughed. "I'm sure you are, Lewis," she said.

Anthony Hamilton looked steadily at his son. "Go-karting isn't like remote-control car racing – it's even more expensive. Neither me nor your mum or Linda have much money."

Lewis looked downcast.

"So, here's the deal," his dad told him. "I'll work at whatever I can to support your racing. In return, you will work harder at school. What do you think? Deal?"

"Deal" replied Lewis, firmly. And they shook hands.

So Lewis worked hard at school, while his dad took two part-time jobs in the evening to pay for his go-kart racing. At the weekends, Lewis, with his dad, practised at their local go-kart racing club, which was called Rye House. Soon, Lewis was ready for his first race.

All go-kart racers have to wear 'black plates' for their first six races, to show that they are beginners. Lewis practised hard for his first 'black plate' race. After watching everyone in practice, Lewis and his dad walked around the track.

"If you're going to win, you've got to brake here," his dad said. "A clear metre later than everyone else. We've still got one day before the race. You can practise more tomorrow."

Lewis practised hard all day. It was getting dark and the circuit was about to close.

"I've got time for a couple more runs," said Lewis.

"Haven't you been round enough?" asked his dad. "You're quicker than all the rest."

"Please, Dad. One or two of the others are doing it."

"OK," said Lewis's dad.

Lewis pushed his car harder and faster than he ever had before. He felt good accelerating down the track. He felt confident braking as late as possible. He was going to be a winner, just like his hero Ayrton Senna.

Then came his final practice lap. He hit the first bend fast and as he did so, another driver suddenly roared up on his inside, clipping Lewis's car. Lewis's car spun wildly round and hit the tyre wall with a sickening thud.

Back in the pits, Lewis's dad had seen it all happen. "Lewis!" he yelled, tearing across to where Lewis's go-kart sat mangled and twisted. "Lewis!"

Chapter Three:

The First Trophy

As Lewis's dad reached the go-kart, he saw Lewis staggering about beside the wreckage. His face was covered in blood.

"Dad!"

"Lewis! Are you OK?"

"It's only a nose bleed. But look at the kart. It's a wreck! Will you be able to fix it?"

"Of course I will," replied his dad.

"In time for the race tomorrow?"

Lewis's dad frowned. "I'll have to, won't I? I'm just so glad you're OK."

That evening, Anthony Hamilton drove to the other side of London to get the parts to fix his son's kart. He worked late into the night and all next morning repairing the damaged vehicle. It was ready just in time.

Back at the track it was a hard race. Most of the competitors were older and bigger than Lewis. But he drove quickly, remembering his dad's advice to brake as late as possible into the bends. Lewis won – and received his first go-kart trophy.

Later that evening, when he was showing his trophy to his step-mum and baby brother, Lewis said: "Ayrton Senna won his first trophy as a boy racing go-karts. Just like me."

Lewis went on to win all five of his 'black plate' go-kart beginnner races. Now he could race his go-kart at circuits all over the country. Every weekend, the Hamiltons piled everything into their box trailer, hitched it up to the family's old car and set off to a go-karting competition.

Often, the weather was dreadful. While Lewis and his dad were out at the track, Linda would sit in the back of the box trailer with baby Nic on her lap. As the cold rain beat down on the roof she made flasks of chicken noodle soup for all the family.

Those weekends were hard, gruelling and uncomfortable. But Lewis knew that this was what he had to do if he was going to become the next Ayrton Senna. And just like the world champion racing driver had when he was a boy, Lewis was winning all of his go-kart races.

But not everybody was happy.

After one race, Lewis was returning to his kart when he found a couple of older, bigger boys blocking his way.

"Think you're Ayrton Senna, do you?" one of them sneered. "Well, listen. You can go and do your karting somewhere else. We can do without your sort here. Got it?" He shoved Lewis, who stumbled backwards.

Later, Lewis told his dad what had happened. "This karting business is a bit more physical than I realised," his dad said. "You've got to learn to handle yourself. Tell you what, I've got a mate who does karate. He can teach you. He can teach me, too."

"You? Why?" asked Lewis.

"While you were being threatened by those lads back there, their dads were warning me off," he said seriously.

So Lewis Hamilton and his dad learnt karate, and Lewis kept on winning races. It seemed nothing could stop his dream.

Then, one afternoon in early May, Lewis had just finished a race when his dad came up to him. His face was anxious and sad.

"Lewis," he said. "I've got some very bad news. Ayrton Senna has just been killed at the San Marino Grand Prix."

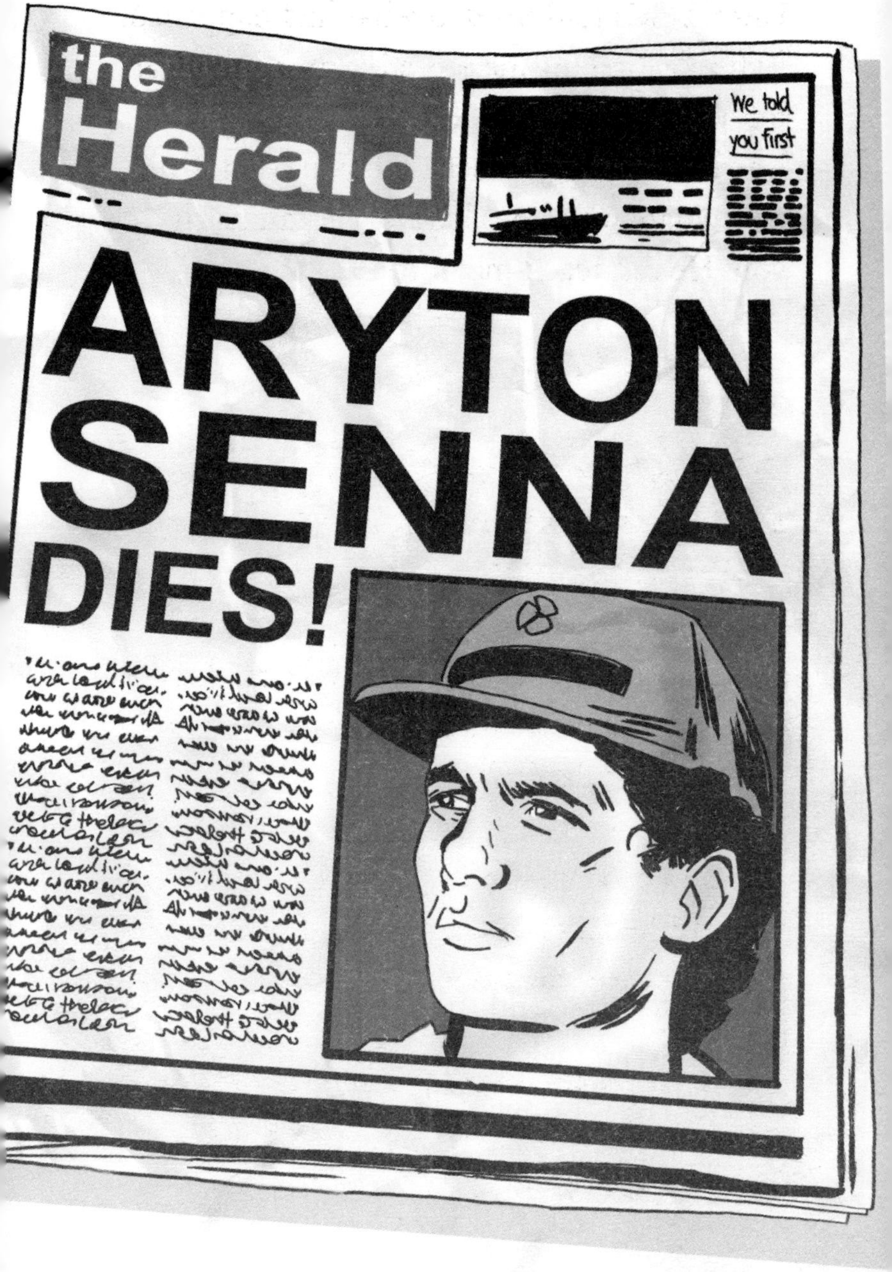

the Herald
We told you first
ARYTON SENNA DIES!

Chapter Four:

The Brother

Lewis walked round the back of the
buildings, and when he was sure nobody was
looking, he sat down and cried. Ayrton
Senna, the man who had inspired his dream,
was dead.

At home later that evening, Lewis found his dad. He was checking the go-kart in the shed at the bottom of the garden.

"I want to give up racing," Lewis said. And before his dad had time to say anything, Lewis ran back inside the house.

His younger brother Nic was playing on the sitting-room floor. Nic had been born with cerebral palsy, which meant he had trouble standing and walking properly. He seemed to sense that Lewis was unhappy and gave him a big, beaming smile. Lewis watched his brother's determination as he grabbed hold of the coffee table and struggled to try and stand up. Walking, running, skipping was what Nic dreamed of, and he was doing his best to try and achieve his dream.

"Nic, you are amazing," murmured Lewis, half to Nic, half to himself.

Nic smiled at him again. It was a smile that seemed to say to Lewis, "look, if I can work hard at trying to stand up so that I can achieve my dream, surely you can work at trying to achieve yours, too?"

"I guess you're right, Nic," whispered Lewis, although his brother had said nothing. It was just what Nic was doing; his determination, his bravery, his smile, that had made Lewis think, 'Yes, motor racing is dangerous. Yes, there will always be accidents and tragedies. But motor racing is *my* dream.' He wouldn't give it up. He would work even harder to become a top driver.

He would do it for Ayrton Senna. He would do it for Nic.

Lewis went back down the garden to the shed, where his dad was still working on the go-kart.

"Dad," said Lewis, "can we go karting again next weekend?"

Chapter Five:

The Awards

The Grosvenor Hotel in Park Lane, London, was packed with men wearing suits and bow ties and women in glittering evening dresses. White-coated waiters served champagne. The occasion was British motor sports' biggest awards ceremony – the annual Autosport Awards.

"And now, the award for the winner of the British Formula Cadet Karting Championship goes to… Lewis Hamilton!"

To roaring cheers, Lewis Hamilton walked up on stage. He was wearing a green velvet jacket borrowed from the boy who had won the award the previous year. Linda had taken the sleeves up to get it to fit. His shiny black shoes were borrowed, too. But that didn't bother Lewis, as with a huge grin, he held the award above his head.

Once the ceremony was over, Lewis went round the room, clutching the autograph book his dad had made for him. He collected autographs from all the famous racing drivers who were there and then his dad said, "Look, over there. That's Ron Dennis, Chairman of the McLaren Group."

Lewis walked up to Ron Dennis and said, "One day I'm going to be a racing driver and I'd like to be in your team."

"Work hard at school and keep that spirit," said Mr Dennis. "Then phone me in nine years and I'll sort you out a deal."

Nine years? It sounded like a lifetime.

The next year, Lewis won the British Kart Championship once more. He went to the Autosport Awards again where Ron Dennis said with a laugh: "What? You again?"

As Lewis progressed through the various classes, the karts got bigger and more expensive. One evening he overheard his dad and Linda talking in the kitchen.

"I don't know how much longer we can keep spending money at this rate," Lewis's dad said. "The car needs a properly qualified mechanic working on it, not me. And qualified mechanics and equipment cost money."

With a heavy heart, Lewis crept upstairs to bed. If his parents couldn't keep supporting his racing, he didn't know what he'd do. Despite his talent, his spirit and all his hard work, might this just be the end of his motor racing dream?

Chapter Six:

The Deal

But Lewis stayed committed to working hard at training, and his parents stayed committed to working hard to pay for his hobby. He won the British Kart Championship for the third year in a row.

Sometimes Ron Dennis would turn up to watch him race. At that year's Autosport Awards, he greeted Lewis almost like an old friend.

A few weeks after the awards, Lewis and his dad stood in the shed, looking at his go-kart. It needed replacement parts, but neither Lewis nor his family knew where the money to pay for them was going to come from. Then Lewis's dad's mobile rang.

"Anthony?"

"Yes… Who's that?"

"Ron Dennis."

"It's Ron Dennis!" Lewis's dad whispered excitedly.

Lewis strained his ears to overhear the conversation.

"How's young Lewis?" asked Ron Dennis.

"Fine," said Lewis's dad.

"How's his kart?"

Lewis's dad looked down at the broken machine. "It's seen better days," he sighed.

"Listen, we'd like to offer Lewis a deal to support his racing. And not in six years' time. Now."

"Now? But Lewis is only 13."

"Yes, but I've seen him race. Your boy has talent and spirit. He works hard. And you can see he's got a dream. A dream to win. And I want him to achieve that dream. I want him to race for the McLaren team."

Eight years later, Lewis Hamilton was racing for the McLaren Formula 1 Team. His first win, at the Canadian Grand Prix, he dedicated to his father.

His next win came at the American Grand Prix.

He dedicated that to his brother, Nic.

43

Fact file
Lewis Hamilton

 Full name: Lewis Carl Hamilton

 Born: Stevenage, Hertfordshire
7th January 1985

1991	Appears on *Blue Peter*, aged 6, as a champion remote-controlled car driver!
1995	Becomes Britain's youngest Formula Cadet champion
1996	McLaren Mercedes 'Champions of the Future' champion, UK 5 Nations champion, Sky TV Kart Masters champion
1998	McLaren Mercedes 'Champions of the Future' runner up. Signs up to McLaren Young Drivers Programme, becomes youngest driver to become contracted to a Formula 1 team
2000	Formula A European champion, World Cup champion, Elf Masters champion
2001	British Formula Renault UK Winter series, fifth in championship
2003	British Formula Renault UK Championship, champion with ten wins
2004	Formula 3 Euroseries, fifth in championship with one win. Winner of Bahrain F3 Superprix
2005	Formula 3 Euroseries, champion with fifteen wins in twenty races. Winner of F3 Masters
2006	GP2 Series champion with five wins
2007	Formula 1. Finishes season as runner up, with four wins, a record for a debut season
2008	Formula 1. Wins British Grand Prix

Monty Panesar

The five boys sitting on the boundary should all have been at school. Instead, they had come to watch a cricket match. Sachin Tendulkar, the greatest batsman in the world, and their number one hero, was playing for the touring Indian side against the local county, Northamptonshire. The boys cheered his every stroke.

After the match, the tallest of the boys opened his kit bag and took out his cricket bat. 'I'm going to get Sachin Tendulkar to sign this,' he announced. He had a dream of becoming a great batsman like Tendulkar. "Well, I don't suppose any of us will ever see him again."

He wasn't to know it; but he was wrong, very wrong indeed.

**Continue reading this story in
DREAM TO WIN: Monty Panesar**

Also by Roy Apps,
published by Franklin Watts:

978 0 7496 7057 3

978 0 7496 7056 6

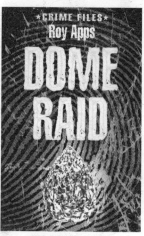

978 0 7496 7054 2

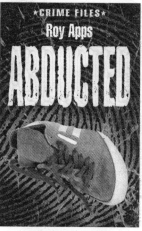

978 0 7496 7053 5